Welcome to the Forest at Night

by Ruth Owen

Ruby Tuesday Books

Published in 2024 by Ruby Tuesday Books Ltd.

Copyright © 2024 Ruby Tuesday Books Ltd.

All rights reserved. No part of this publication may be reproduced in whole or in part, stored in any retrieval system, or transmitted in any form or by any means, electronic, mechanical, photocopying, recording, or otherwise, without written permission from the publisher.

Editor: Ruth Owen
Design and Production: Alix Wood

Photo credits
Alamy: 13 (Max Allen); 18 (Malcolm Schuyl); 23L (Corina Daniela Obertas); Nature Picture Library: 10 (Andy Sands); 13R (Kevin J Keatley); 15B (Kim Taylor); 17 (Kim Taylor); 19 (Alex Hyde); 24 (Michael Durham); 27B (Philippe Clement); 29 (Andrew Cooper); Shutterstock: Cover (wewi-creative and Rudmer Zwerver); 2 (Sonsedska Yuliia); 3 (Rudmer Zwerver, Eric Isselee, Bernatskaia Oksana and Jiang Hongyan); 4L (Rudmer Zwerver); 4R (D. Kucharski K. Kucharska); 5L (Gerald A. DeBoer); 5 (Gallinago Media); 6L (antoniocm); 6R (Martin Prochazkacz); 8L (S. Zykov); 8R (Dave M Hunt Photography); 9 (Cezary Korkosz); 11 (Kichigin); 12 (Danita Delimont); 14 (Igor Krasilov); 15T (Back Garden Photography); 16 (Andrew M. Allport); 20–21 (slow motiongli); 22 (Rudmer Zwerver); 23R (kvikto); 24 (Evelyn D. Harrison); 25 (Robert Vandenbeg); 28 (Astrid Gast and Vinokurov Alexandr); 29 (Karen Hogan); 30 (Bernatskaia Oksana, IrinaK, slow motiongli, Rudmer Zwerver, azure 1, Jiang Hongyan and Andrew M. Allport); 31 (Nikolay 007, Tiffany K, sezer66 and Chanita Chokchaikul; Superstock: 7 (Clickalps SRLs/age fotostock); 25 (Sohns/imageBROKER); 26 (Bernd Rohrschneider/age fotostock); 27T (Regis Cavignaux/Biosphoto).

Library of Congress Control Number: 2023903513
Print (Hardback) ISBN 978-1-78856-303-1
Print (Paperback) ISBN 978-1-78856-304-8
ePub ISBN 978-1-78856-306-2

Published in Minneapolis, MN
Printed in the United States

www.rubytuesdaybooks.com

Contents

Welcome to the Forest at Night 4

A Silent Hunter 6

Forest Floor Foraging 8

Drip, Drip, Drop 10

What's for Dinner? 12

Glowing and Changing 14

Taking Flight 16

A Night-Time Feast 18

Napping the Day Away 20

A Bat's Busy Night 22

Tree Hole Homes 24

Hungry Owlets 26

Morning in the Forest 28

A Night-Time Forest Food Web 30

Glossary 31

Index 32

Words shown in **bold** in the text are explained in the glossary.

Welcome to the Forest at Night

A forest **habitat** is home to trees and other plants.

Animals such as **insects**, birds, and **mammals** live there, too.

A forest is a type of ecosystem. An ecosystem includes all the living things in an area. It also includes non-living things such as rain and soil. Everything in an ecosystem has its own part to play.

Long-eared bat

Elephant hawkmoth

The plants and animals get everything they need to survive from the forest.

Some forest animals are **nocturnal**.

This means they are mostly active at night.

Raccoon kits

What happens in this habitat when darkness falls? Welcome to the forest at night!

A Silent Hunter

As the Sun sets, a sound floats through the trees.

Hoo hoo. Hoo hoooo.

It's a male tawny owl, perched high on a tree branch.

Kew-wick. Kew-wick. The owl's **mate** answers him.

She is waiting at their tree-hole nest.

Male tawny owl

Nest hole

Female tawny owl

Suddenly, the male owl hears a soft rustling in the leaves on the ground.

He drops silently to the forest floor and grabs a mouse.

Male tawny owl

Mouse

A tawny owl can hear 10 times better than a human! It uses its hearing and eyesight to hunt mice, voles, and shrews.

Then he carries the **prey** back to his mate at their nest.

Who is snuffling through dead leaves on the forest floor?

Forest Floor Foraging

As night falls, a forest floor comes alive!

Tiny **rodents**, such as wood mice, voles, and shrews, scuttle through the dead leaves.

Bank vole

Berries

Wood mouse

A bank vole climbs from the underground burrow that she dug in the soft forest soil.

She **forages** for nuts and berries to eat.

Common shrews live in forests in Europe. They are just 2 inches (5 cm) long. This little rodent will eat an earthworm that's twice the length of its own body!

A shrew snuffles through the **leaf litter**, sniffing with its long nose for earthworms, spiders, and insects.

Shrew

Earthworm

How do you think the forest plants and animals get water?

Drip, Drip, Drop

Big drops of rain start to fall on the forest.

The water soaks into the soil, and the roots of the trees suck it up.

Wood mouse

Puddle

Shallow dips in the ground become puddles where the forest animals can drink.

The raindrops hit a puffball **fungus**, making it puff millions of **spores** into the air.

The spores are so small, hundreds could fit on the period at the end of this sentence.

Each tiny spore contains everything that's needed to grow a new puffball.

Spores

Puffball fungus

A puffball's root-like hyphae spread through dead leaves and wood. The hyphae help break down the dead material. This makes it rot faster and become new soil.

What hungry forest resident is waiting for the rain to stop?

What's for Dinner?

Opossum

When the rain stops, an opossum leaves her den.

She drinks rainwater from a small pond that has formed under the trees.

Then it's time to get sniffing for food.

Opossums are omnivores, which means they eat both meat and plants. They are also scavengers that eat the dead bodies of other animals.

The opossum forages for earthworms, slugs, snails, insects, birds, eggs, mice, frogs, lizards, and even snakes.

She also feeds on berries, nuts, and seeds.

All the opossum's favorite foods can be found in her forest habitat.

An opossum eating a dead raccoon in winter

Who is lighting up the night-time forest?

Glowing and Changing

By day, a female glow-worm hides from hungry **predators** in the forest soil.

But at night, she climbs to a high point on a plant and glows green!

Glow-worm

Bioluminescence

A glow-worm is not actually a worm—it's a type of beetle. The light is called bioluminescence. It's made by special substances and oxygen inside the beetle's body.

Male glow-worms fly through the forest looking for females.

The female makes her light to attract a mate.

Tonight, another forest insect is stirring.

Last autumn, this little animal was a hungry, leaf-eating caterpillar.

Then it became a **pupa**. Now, inside its tough outer case, its body has completely changed.

What night-time insect do you think the pupa has become?

Taking Flight

The pupa spent the winter hidden in leaf litter on the forest floor.

Now, it has transformed into an elephant hawkmoth.

The moth climbs from its pupa case and spreads its wings.

Elephant hawkmoth

Soon, the moth is ready to take flight.

An elephant hawkmoth can see in the dark and has a good sense of smell.

Honeysuckle flowers

It uses these senses to search for food at night.

Elephant hawkmoths get their name because their caterpillars look like an elephant's trunk. As adults, these moths can beat their wings quickly to hover in one place—just like a hawk!

What kind of food do you think an elephant hawkmoth eats?

A Night-Time Feast

A beautiful smell floats through a dark forest—honeysuckle!

The smell attracts moths that drink sweet nectar from the flowers with their long, straw-like tongues.

Honeysuckle flower

Elephant hawkmoth feeding

Elephant hawkmoth

Eye

Pollen

Curled-up tongue

As moths and other insects visit honeysuckle flowers, dusty pollen sticks to their bodies. Then the insects carry the pollen from flower to flower. This helps the honeysuckle flowers make seeds.

Honeysuckle plants climb up and wind around tree trunks and branches.

The scent of their flowers gets stronger at night.

How might the tangled stems of honeysuckle plants be helpful to another tiny forest animal?

Napping the Day Away

A little dormouse is shredding up the bark on the stems of a honeysuckle plant.

Then she uses the bark to weave a round nest.

Dormice are found in forests in Europe. Their name comes from the French word *dormir*, which means "to sleep." They spend about three-quarters of their lives asleep.

She will give birth to her babies and spend the day sleeping in the nest.

Dormouse nest

At night, the dormouse climbs through the trees, foraging for food.

She eats honeysuckle flowers and berries, blackberries, nuts, pollen, and insects.

Berry

What tiny nocturnal mammal is hunting for flying insects?

A Bat's Busy Night

A tiny bat flies here and there, grabbing insects in her mouth.

She eats about 3,000 moths and other insects every night!

Wrist
Fingers
Arm
Pipistrelle bat
Arm
Wing
Furry body

An adult pipistrelle bat weighs the same as a nickel. With its wings folded, it could fit inside this circle.

During the day, the bat rests by hanging upside-down inside the hollow trunk of an old tree.

Lots of female bats have gathered together in this safe place.

Each one has given birth to a tiny pup.

A pipistrelle bat pup on a scientist's finger

When it's time to hunt, the mother bats leave their pups in a group, inside the tree.

Hollow tree trunk

What other nocturnal animals make their homes in a forest's trees?

Tree Hole Homes

The opossum has made a den in the trunk of an old, fallen tree.

She used her long, bendy tail to drag leaves and grass into the den to make a soft bed.

Inside, she gave birth to six tiny babies, called joeys.

Fallen tree

Opossum

Den entrance

Newborn opossums live in a pouch on their mother's tummy. When they are about three months old, they leave the pouch and ride on her back.

Joey

Mother opossum

A mother raccoon and her kits spend their days sleeping in their tree hole den.

At night, the mother raccoon forages for nuts, berries, insects, eggs, rodents, and frogs.

Mother raccoon

Raccoon kit

The kits climb and swing in the trees, discovering what their little bodies can do!

Hoo hoo is exploring the trees in the night-time forest?

25

Hungry Owlets

The male and female tawny owls are raising two chicks.

Tonight, the young owlets have left the family's tree hole nest.

They walk, climb, and jump through the trees, fluttering their little wings.

This behavior is known as branching.

Owlet

Mouse

Owlet

Mouse

A mouse's jawbone and teeth

Owl pellet

The busy mother and father owls bring the owlets mice to eat.

Just like their parents, the owlets swallow their food whole!

An owl swallows the fur, bones, and teeth of its prey. A few hours after eating, the owl spits up this unwanted stuff in a lump called an owl pellet.

What happens in the forest when daytime comes?

Morning in the Forest

As morning comes, the forest's nocturnal animals seem to disappear.

But it's possible to spot signs of their night-time activities.

Raccoon tracks next to a puddle

Entrance to an underground burrow dug by a wood mouse

And sometimes it's possible to spot where they are hiding.

Eastern screech owl

Owls spend the day resting in tree holes or on branches. Eastern screech owls can be very difficult to see because their feathers are such good camouflage against tree bark.

When the Sun sets, the night-time forest will come alive again.

A Night-Time Forest Food Web

A food web shows who eats who in a habitat.

This food web shows the connections between some of the nocturnal animals in a forest.

Plants can make the food they need for energy inside themselves. To do this, they need sunlight.

The arrows mean: **eaten by**

Glossary

forage
To search for food in the area where you live.

fungus
A living thing, such as a mushroom, toadstool, or type of mold.

habitat
The place where a living thing, such as a plant or animal, makes its home. A forest or garden is a type of habitat.

insect
A small animal with six legs, a body in three main parts, and a tough, outer shell called an exoskeleton.

leaf litter
Dead plant material, such as leaves and twigs, that has fallen to the ground.

mammal
A warm-blooded animal that has a skeleton and fur or hair. Mammals breathe air with lungs and give birth to live babies.

mate
An animal's partner with which it has young.

nocturnal
Active at night.

predator
An animal that hunts and eats other animals.

prey
An animal that is hunted and eaten by other animals.

pupa
The stage in an insect's life between being a larva and becoming an adult.

rodent
A mammal with extra-large front teeth that never stop growing. This animal group includes mice, rats, and hamsters.

spore
A tiny part of a fungus, and some types of plants, that can grow into a new living thing.

Index

B
bats 4, 22–23, 30
bioluminescence 14

C
caterpillars 15, 17

D
dormice 20–21

E
earthworms 9, 13, 30
elephant hawkmoths 4, 15, 16–17, 18–19, 30

F
fungi 11

G
glow-worms 14

H
honeysuckles 17, 18–19, 20–21

I
insects 4, 9, 13, 14–15, 16–17, 18–19, 21, 22, 25, 30

M
mice 7, 8, 10, 13, 26–27, 28, 30

O
opossums 12–13, 24, 30
owls 6–7, 26–27, 29, 30

P
plants 4, 9, 10–11, 13, 14, 17, 18–19, 20–21, 23, 24–25, 30
pupae 15, 16

R
raccoons 5, 13, 25, 28
rain 4, 10–11, 12

S
shrews 7, 8–9, 30

V
voles 7, 8

W
worms 9, 13, 30

Imperial Public Library
PO BOX 307
Imperial, TX 79743